CELEBRATING OUR LOVE

MARRIAGE ACTIVITY BOOK

Welcome To Your Journey of Celebrating Your Love Together

What's in this book?

Celebrating Our Love is filled with carefully selected activities that can help you and your spouse celebrate what you cherish about your marriage, craft new bonding rituals and experiences that encourage you to continue to support each other with deep, loving respect, and rejoice in the future you can plan together.

Do we complete the activities in the order they appear in the book?

Just as your marriage is a journey, so this book is organized like a thoughtfully planned journey. You can do the activities in any order, but please recognize that a few activities are dependent upon activities that are introduced earlier in the book.

You can also redo many of the activities again and again to continue celebrating your love through these activities.

What else should we know?

Challenge yourself and each other to work together to complete the activities in this book. Practices similar to some of the activities in this book have been associated with couples with strong, loving relationships.

Important warning: The books in the Drawing Closer Together™ series are for informational purposes only. The books are not intended to serve as any form of or substitute for marriage, couple, or individual therapy or medical treatment. Seek professional help immediately for any such concerns that arise in general or during the course of completing the activities in this book.

Ok, we're ready.

Excellent. Let's get you and your spouse started on the Celebrating Your Love journey.

FIFTY FUN BONDING ACTIVITIES TO HELP
MARRIED COUPLES GROW CLOSER TOGETHER

CELEBRATING
OUR LOVE

MARRIAGE ACTIVITY BOOK

ELLE DAHLMAN, M. A.

**INWARD
VISTAS**

Celebrating Our Love Marriage Activity Book

This is a Drawing Closer Together™ book Published by Inward Vistas

Copyright © 2016 Inward Vistas LLC

This edition printed in 2016 by
Inward Vistas LLC,
2906 Central Avenue, Suite 252,
Evanston, Illinois 60201

Notice of Rights

Notice of Liability

The information in this book is distributed on an "As Is" basis, without any warranty for entertainment purposes only. While every precaution has been taken in the development of the book, neither the author nor Inward Vistas LLC shall have any liability to any person or entity with respect to any loss or damage caused or alleged to be caused directly or indirectly by the instructions contained in this book.

The content of the book is not intended and does not provide any form of medical, psychological, or psychiatric diagnosis or treatment or counseling for a particular condition. It is not intended to serve as a replacement, in part or in total, for a health care, psychology, or psychiatric professional. Consultation with such a professional is recommended to answer concerns or provide professional diagnosis or treatment.

Trademarks

Inward Vistas, Drawing Closer TogetherTM and Celebrating Our Love Marriage Activity Book are trademarks of Inward Vistas LLC. Rather than place a trademark symbol by each instance of these trademarked names, Inward Vistas LLC indicates with this statement that each instance is a trademarked usage of that term.

ISBN: 1-945037-00-8   ISBN 13: 978-1-945037-00-9

10 9 8 7 6 5 4 3 2 1

Printed and bound in the United States of America.

CELEBRATING
OUR LOVE

Table of Contents

Creating a sense of tranquility will help you begin your journey of celebrating your love. Start, then, with a deep relaxation exercise that can calm your mind and body.

Get comfortable and begin taking in deep breaths. Inhale in, expanding your diaphragm (above your stomach), then slowly exhaling, pushing air out of your diaphragm area.

You can repeat this exercise together before doing the activities in other sections of this book or whenever you're feeling stressed.

Now it's time to move around a bit. Start by stretching your bodies, perhaps by stretching your neck and arms, then waist and legs. Continue to stretch until you both feel ready to move.

If you know yoga poses, this would be good time to share a few gentle yoga poses with your spouse.

Did you know that stretching exercises like these promote relaxation and relief from stress?

Now you are going to play Follow the Leader. Choose one of you to start as the leader. The leader will then form his or her body into a pose or perform a series of movements.

The other one will follow, and when you are able to copy your spouse's movements, then you become the leader, and you will create a more challenging set of movements for your partner to copy.

Keep going until both of you feel relaxed and loose.

A great way to connect with your spouse is to touch his or her body in a loving way.

Give each other a hand or back message, or even a full body massage. Then try a facial with a warm washcloth or a foot massage that starts with a warm soak followed by a tender foot rub.

End with a shared shower featuring lots of sudsy rubdowns.

Think back on when you were first getting to know your spouse. Write below some things that first attracted you to him or her.

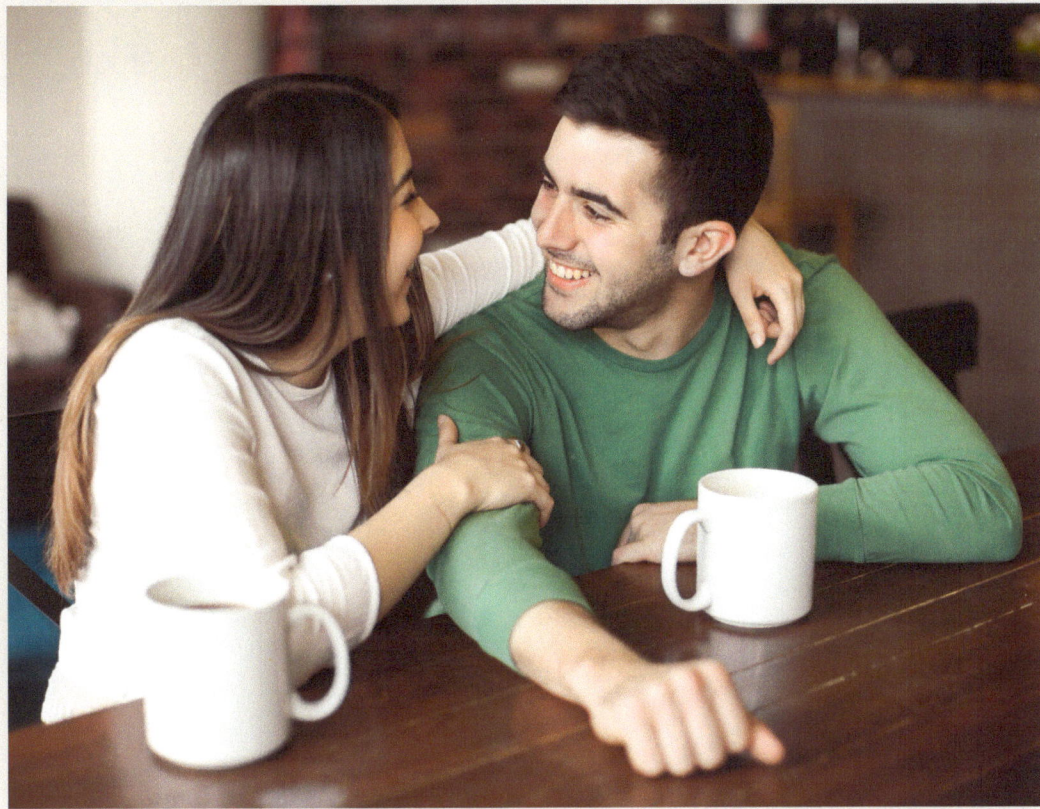

_____

_____

_____

_____

Your attraction may change over time. Share something that attracts you these days to your spouse.

Write a recollection of how your spouse won your heart, using a fairytale writing style. Cast yourselves as a prince and princess in the story.

Start your story with "Once upon a time ..." or "There once was a ..." Try to also use a fairytale ending, such as "... and we lived happily ever after" or "... and that is how it is to this day" to end your fairytale.

_____

_____

_____

_____

_____

_____

_____

Now read your story to your partner and enjoy remembering the story with a new slant.

Do you recall your wedding vows?

Find a copy of your wedding vows and read them each other.

Update your vows together if you'd like to make some changes to them.

Consider having a small ceremony or a dinner out during which you renew your vows to each other.

Couples often spend a fair amount of time picking a wedding song with just the right meaning, so it is worth listening to it from time to time throughout your life together.

Start by finding a recording of your wedding song. Then play the song and dance to it as you did on your wedding night.

Do you have any clothing from your wedding? Wear it while you dance to relive the memory.

Cherishing Our Past

Recalling milestones in your relationship can be heartwarming and help you reminisce about good times you've enjoyed together.

Find your wedding album or an album of family pictures and spend some going through it together.

Pick out a favorite photo in the album and share why you enjoy recalling that event.

Think back on a funny event that the two of you would enjoy reminiscing about together.

Write about the sequence of events leading up to the event, including what made it funny. Then enjoy a good laugh together as you share your recollections.

My Funny Story

You can download additional copies at http://bit.ly/2d0K4YW.

Managing your finances together is an important part of being able to maintain a happy relationship.

Think about one financial goal the two of you have already achieved.

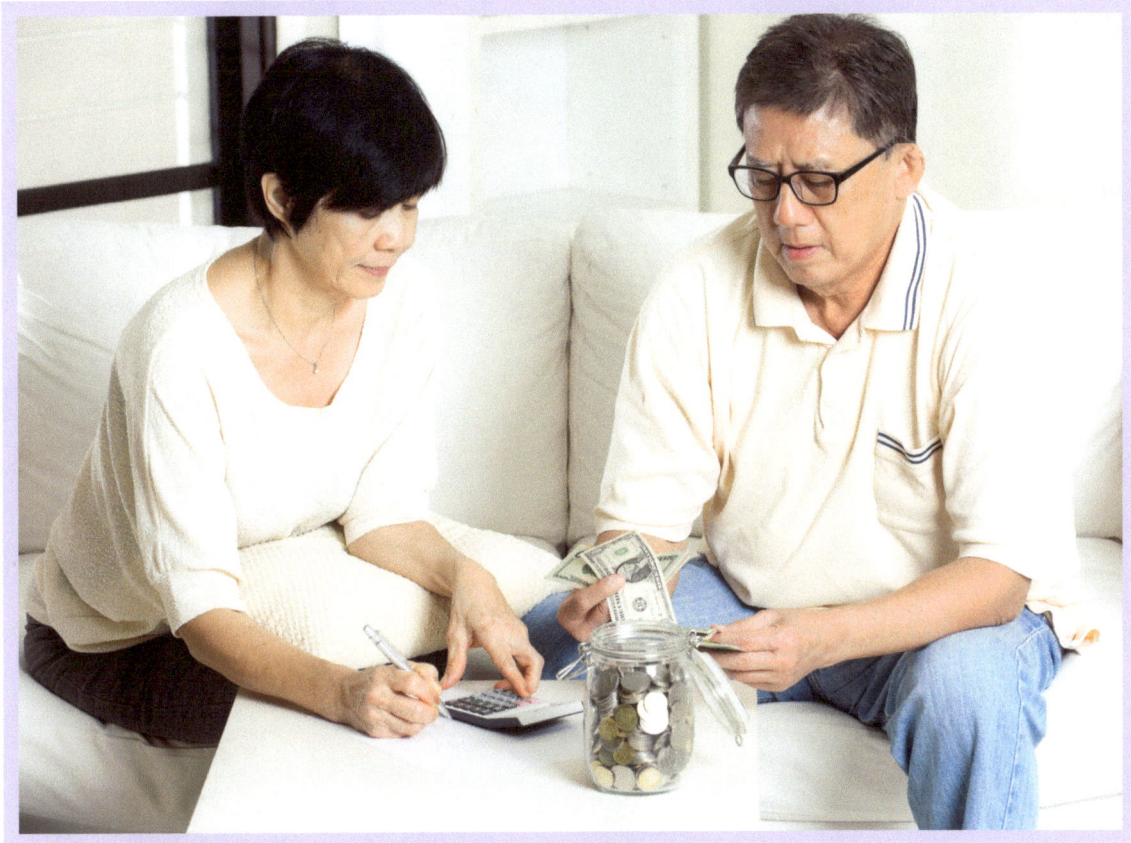

Talk about one change that you can make together to advance your financial situation now.

What do you feel should be the current purpose of your marriage?

Write your answer on the heart-shaped pad below.

Talk together about how close the current state of your marriage is to the purpose you envision.

Checking the State of Our Union

Just as the US president reflects on the state of the country with an annual State of the Union speech, you can write a State of Our Union document reflecting on the state of your marriage.

Work together on a State of Our Union. The form below is just a sample. Use the full page State of Our Union form on the next page for your answers.

The State of Our Union

Date: _____

The best parts of our marriage are

We can get better at

Going forward, we should

You can download additional copies at http://bit.ly/2d0K4YW.

The State of Our Union

Date: _____

The best parts of our marriage are

We can get better at

Going forward, we should

Do you have a hobby that your partner doesn't share? Spend a few minutes showing your partner how one does your hobby.

When you are the spouse being shown the hobby, welcome the chance to enter your partner's world to learn about something he or she enjoys doing as a way to gain more appreciation of how your partner chooses to spend some of his or her time.

Appreciating how your spouse chooses to spend free time practicing hobbies can show your respect for his or her interests.

Next up, choose an exercise or play a sport together that you both enjoy.

Working out together is an excellent way to help each other achieve your fitness goals.

Having Fun Together

Here's a fun game you'll enjoy playing together.

It's called the Alphabet List game. Pick a category like songs, sports, movies, cities, or food. Then take turns naming something in the category you chose that starts with the letters of the alphabet, *in alphabetical order* from A to Z.

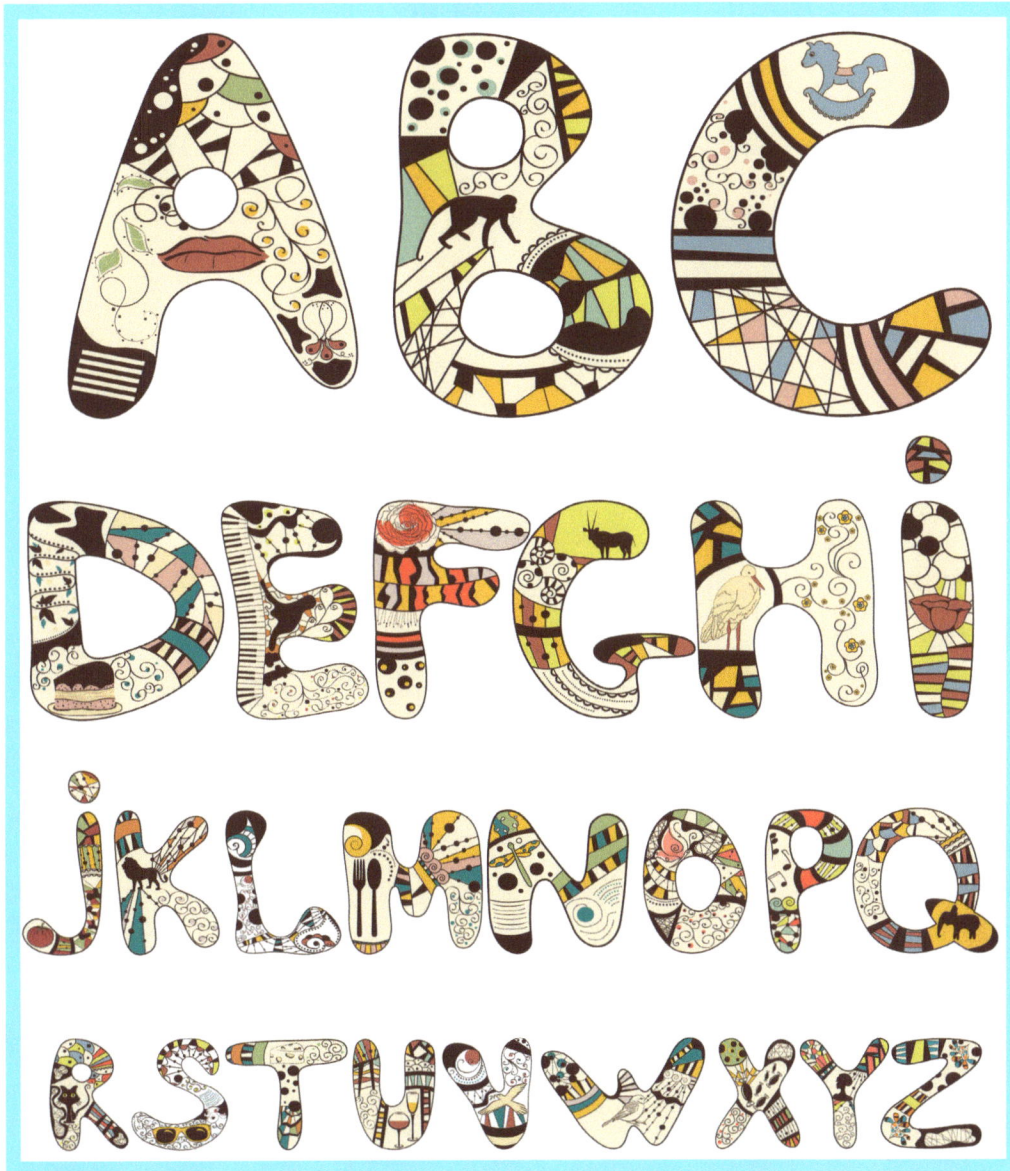

Help each other out if you are stuck naming an object for a letter.

Cooking together is a great recipe for a happy marriage.

You can make healthy meals and enjoy time together while producing a tasty reward – a fine meal.

You can take your time together to an even higher level by making an extra portion for a nearby friend or relative and generously inviting them over for dinner.

Share what you enjoyed about working together in the kitchen as you enjoy the meal you made together.

Yes, it is true – couples who play together stay together!

So schedule a play date – with each other. Borrow some of your kids' toys or go to a gaming facility to bowl, play miniature golf, or enjoy some other zany activity.

Share with your spouse the toys you enjoyed playing with most as a child. See if you can borrow or obtain those toys for your next playdate.

Did you know that the number of times couples laugh together tends to decline as they age? Don't let this happen to you!

Keep the laughter alive by finding a favorite recording of a comedian you enjoy and listening to it together.

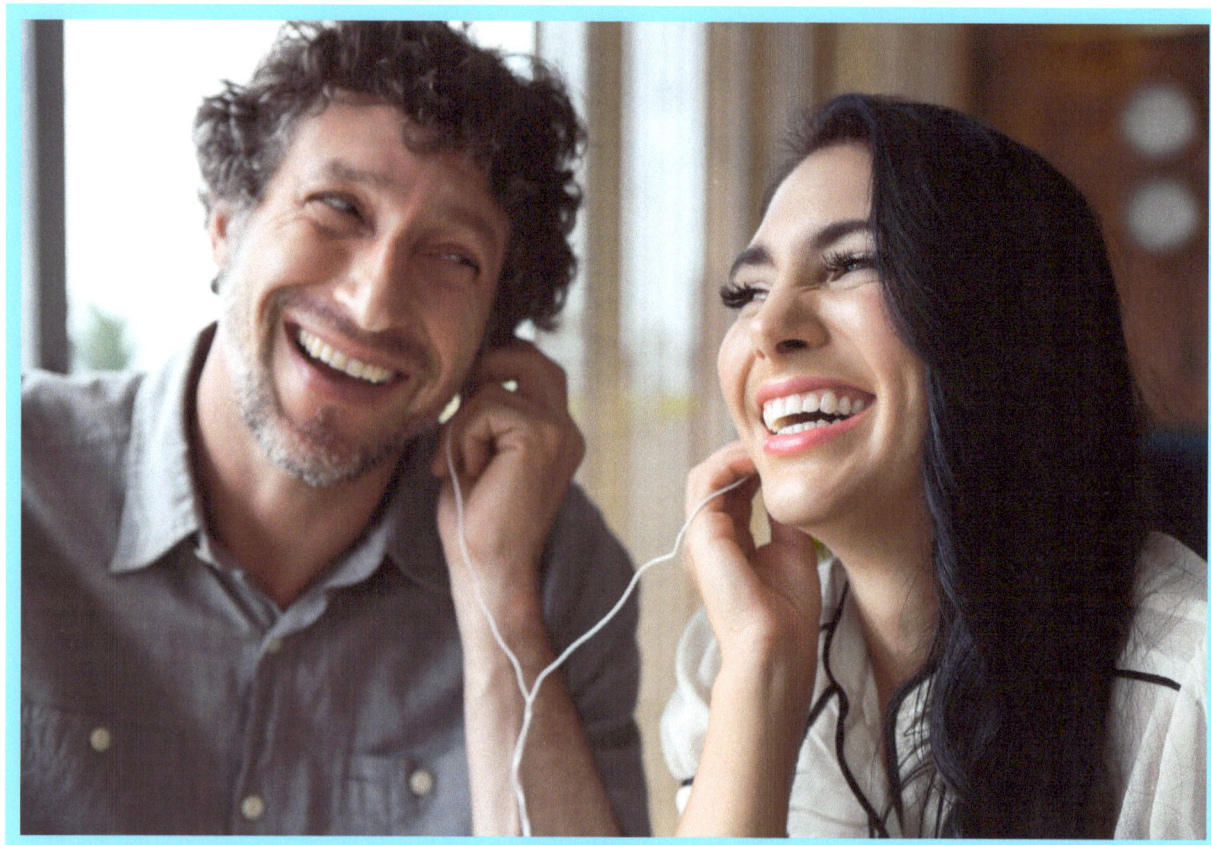

Figure out ways you can schedule a date filled with laughter, such as going to a comedy club or watching comedians online.

Here's a surprising way to experience immense pleasure – simply help others through volunteer work.

Get together with your spouse and find a volunteer activity you can do together, whether it's an informal way to help someone or as part of an organization.

Finding an activity that is linked to your interests and physical capabilities may help you stick with it.

Take a stroll outside to enjoy the invigorating warmth of a brisk walk together. You'll find that a walk outside can give you a real positive boost even in the middle of winter.

Holding hands while you walk can also give you an added lift.

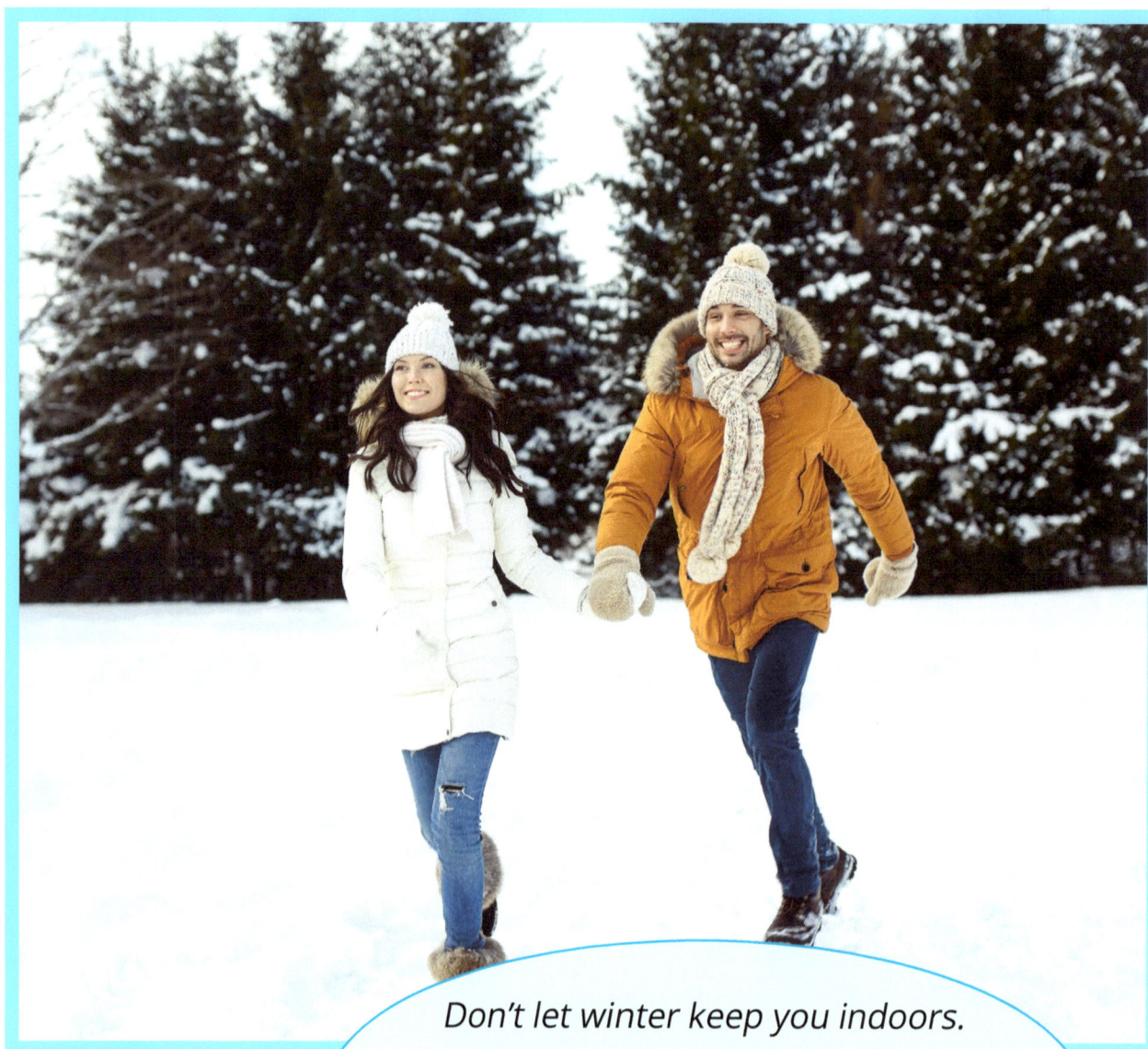

Don't let winter keep you indoors. Good vibes are waiting for you and your spouse outside during all four seasons.

Now, instead of making the usual To Do list to give to your spouse, together create a joint Honey Let's Do Together list of tasks you can do with each other. You'll find that working together to improve your living environment can be much more fun than doing it alone.

A full page worksheet is on the following page.

Honey Let's Do Together List

Our Tasks   Completed

_____ ☐

_____ ☐

_____ ☐

_____ ☐

You can download additional copies at
http://bit.ly/2d0K4YW

Honey Let's Do Together List

Our Tasks	Completed
_____	☐
_____	☐
_____	☐
_____	☐
_____	☐
_____	☐
_____	☐
_____	☐
_____	☐
_____	☐

Complete one of the Honey Let's Do Together tasks on the list you just made. Reward each other with a small treat when you finish the task.

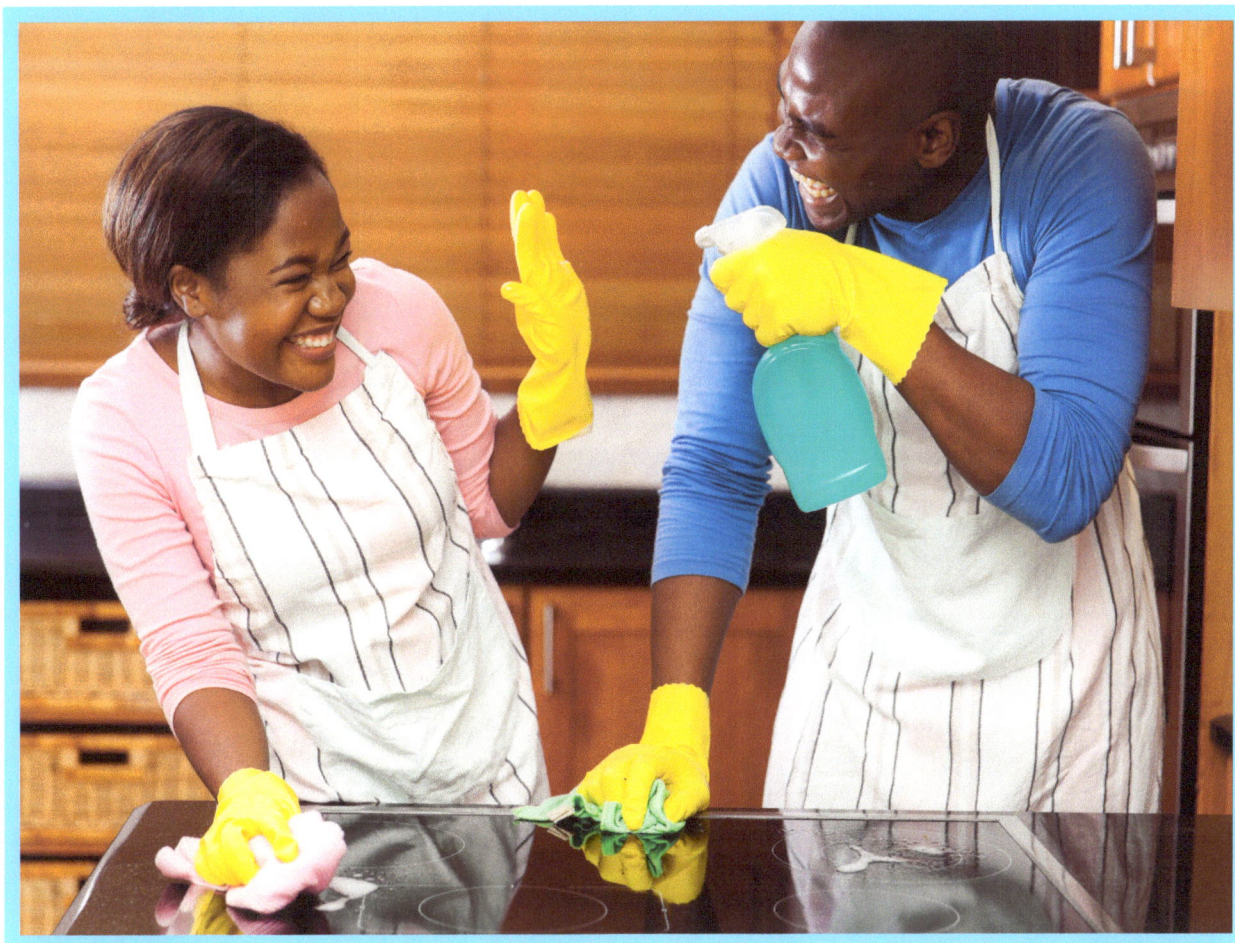

Now that you've completed one task from your list, talk about which task the two of you will tackle next.

Spending time with other couples who show loving behavior toward each other can set a positive example for your relationship.

Go out with another couple and have an entertaining experience together that is new for each of you.

Talk first about which couple you would like to go out with and what activity you could do together.

Having Fun Together

Try something wild, outside your comfort zone.

Okay, maybe jumping out of a plane is *way* too far outside your comfort zone, but trying something new, outside your routine, with your spouse can increase your sense of marital happiness.

Commit to making and completing a list of new activities that are at least a few steps outside of each of your comfort zones.

Wouldn't it be nice to find a love note that your spouse had written to you as you go about your day?

Write a brief note of appreciation and love to your spouse on one of the heart-shaped notes place it where he or she is likely to find it in the next day or two.

You can download additional copies at http://bit.ly/2d0K4YW.

Letting your spouse know you are thinking of him or her during the day is a touching way to show you care.

If he or she is reachable via text message when you're apart, try sending a text. You could use one of the starter messages below.

Thank you for ...

Let's stay up tonight and ...

BTW, I liked how you ...

Just saying hi

I just heard a really interesting ...

How's it going?

Of course, you'll need to be mindful about their availability to text during the day.

We each have a need to be feel understood, and a marriage is a key place to have that need fulfilled.

Take time now to tell each other a story about a difficult situation you recently faced.

The key is that when you are the listener, actively listen and understand your spouse's feelings about the situation.

Then switch roles so that now you are the storyteller or listener.

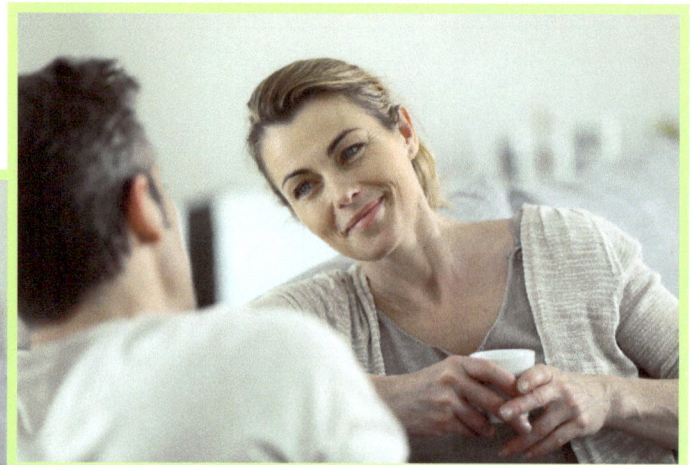

After you have each shared your stories, take turns putting yourself in your spouse's shoes and provide a supportive reaction to their story.

Schedule a Romantic Movie Festival for you and your spouse. Each week pick out a romantic movie and watch it together.

The key is to chat about what the couples in the movies are doing well to promote a happy relationship. Also, keep an eye on how often one of the romantic leads responds to the other's words and actions in the movie.

Pick out your next movie and the date when you'll watch it together after the movie ends.

Do you have a ritual way to greet each other when you are back together again at the end of a workday?

If not, spend a few minutes together discussing how you would like to greet each other. A simple hug, a deep kiss, a few minutes cuddling or recounting the events of your day can help you reconnect.

Practice the ways you'll reconnect at the end of a workday, just so you are both comfortable with them before show time at the end of your next workday.

Communicating Our Love

Do you have a ritual way to end the day with your spouse?

If not, pick a few activities that some spouses use to end their day together from the list below.

Circle the ones you want to use on the following page and hang it up in your bedroom or somewhere where you both will see it.

1. Say goodnight to your tech devices by turning them off or down.

2. Settle any arguments or agree to discuss them the next day.

3. Give a massage.

4. Snuggle up together.

5. Indicate any desires about intimacy during the night.

6. Think about spirituality together

7. Kiss each other good night.

8. Say "I love you" right before you go to sleep.

You can download additional copies at http://bit.ly/2d0K4YW.

Our Good Night Rituals

Date: _____

1

2

3

4

5

6

7

8

Communicating Our Love

What's a particularly yucky household task your spouse performs?

Complete the certificates on the next page to show him or her your appreciation of their willingness to do that task.

Certificate of Appreciation

Awarded to

_____

In recognition of

_____

_____   _____
Awarded by   Date

You can also download additional copies at http://bit.ly/2d0K4YW.

Certificate of Appreciation

Awarded to

_____

In recognition of

_____

_____   _____

Awarded by   Date

Certificate of Appreciation

Awarded to

_____

In recognition of

_____

_____   _____

Awarded by   Date

Write about a memorable moment when your partner totally exceeded your wildest expectations by doing something really special for you.

Share what your spouse's actions demonstrated to you about his or her love for you.

Sometimes our spouse gives us encouragement when we are hesitating to take the first steps toward achieving one of our goals.

Write a description of one way your partner has supported your efforts to achieve one of your goals.

Ponder whether there is a way you can help your spouse with one of his or her current goals, then share your idea with your spouse.

Appreciating Each Other

Write the headline for a recent accomplishment that your spouse achieved such as a career milestone, exercise success, or personal goal.

Then show each other the headline you wrote for them.

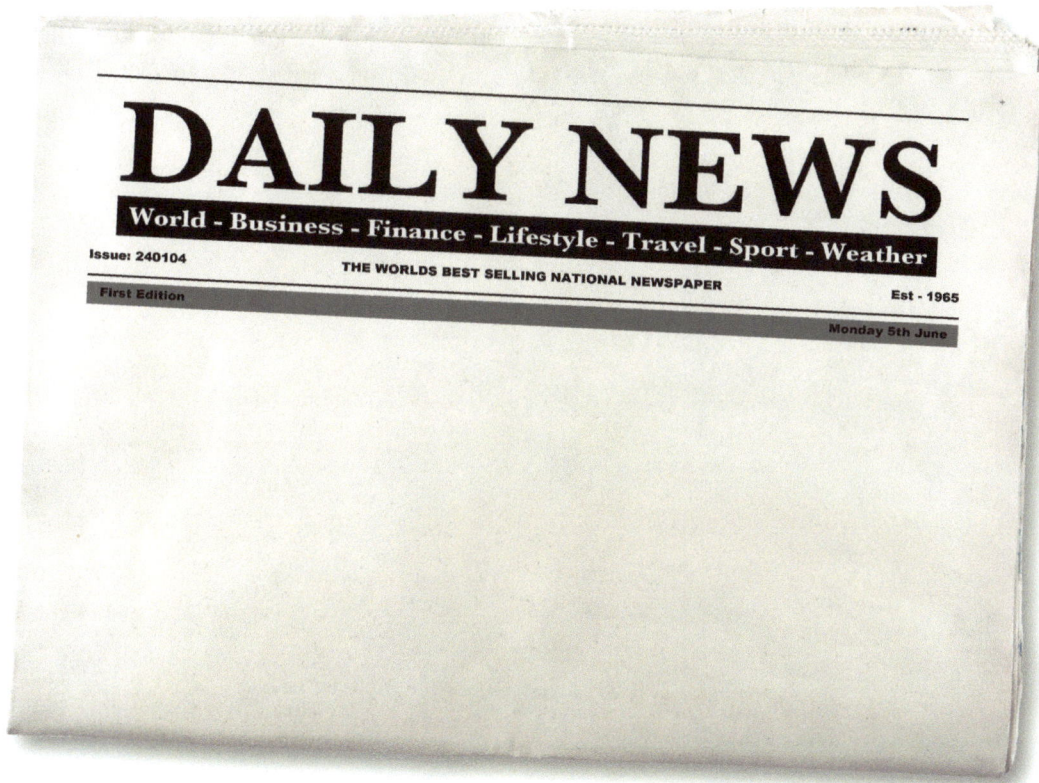

DAILY NEWS

World - Business - Finance - Lifestyle - Travel - Sport - Weather

Issue: 240104

THE WORLDS BEST SELLING NATIONAL NEWSPAPER

First Edition

Est - 1965

Monday 5th June

Recognizing your spouse's accomplishments can let him or her know that you appreciate all the hard work it took to improve.

Every marriage can hit roadblocks such as financial, health, or parenting problems. What is one challenge that you faced together and worked together to solve?

Write on the plaque, "We survived..." and finish the sentence on the plaque with a brief description of the challenge the two of you survived.

Surviving adversity can serve as proof that your marriage can survive most anything.

Appreciating Each Other

Think of a brand-new way to show that you cherish your spouse.

Keep your idea a mystery to your spouse but show it by doing it on a regular basis.

Surprise! You and your spouse have just been selected to appear on the *World's Biggest Flirt* television show.

Well, at least pretend you were chosen by sitting next to each other and taking turns flirting with each other.

Try to flirt with your spouse on a regular basis. And if you are being flirted, showing your appreciation by encouraging their efforts.

Being Intimate Together

Do you have favorite discreet emojis on your phone you send to each other when you are apart and thinking about being intimate?

If so, draw your favorite emoji that you use to suggest being intimate later in the bubble below.

If you don't have a set of discreet emojis for this, scroll through the emojis on your phones together and draw a few emojis that you will send to each other when the thought crosses your mind.

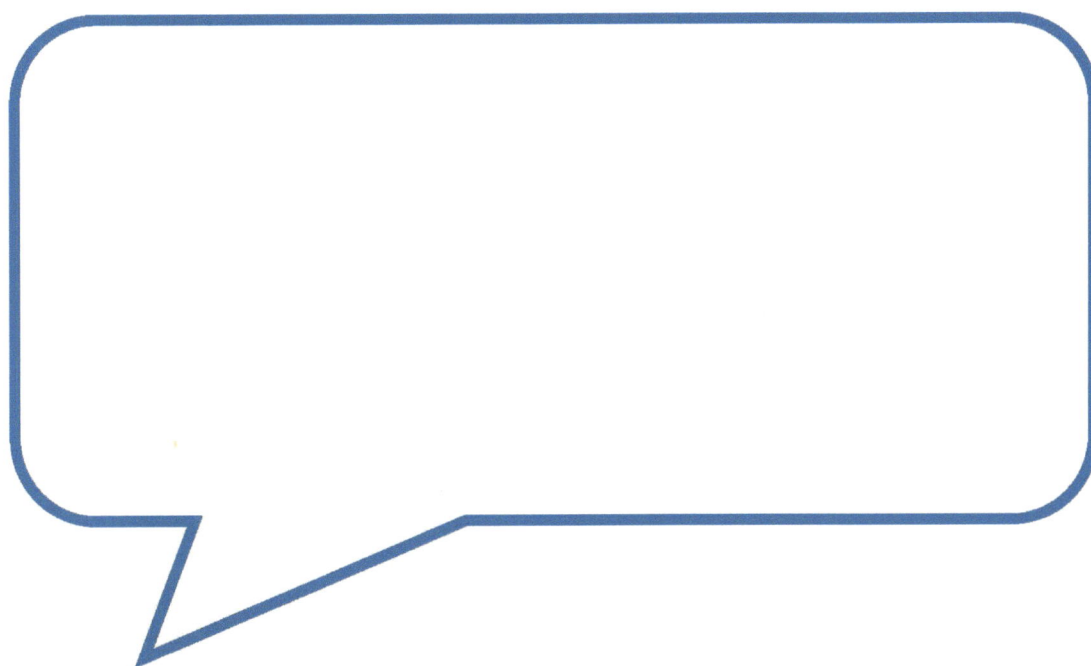

When the thought occurs to you, go ahead and text the emoji you agreed would be your secret code.

Do you have a set of favorite songs that you play during your intimate moments together?

Make a mixtape playlist of romantic songs the two of you would enjoy listening to together to get in the mood.

Start up the playlist the next time you want to get intimate with your spouse. Romantic music can get things going.

Being Intimate Together

Get ready to pucker up. Have you fallen out of the kissing habit with your spouse?

Try getting back into the habit by first starting with brief kisses and making them last longer each time.

Research has shown that including kissing when you are with your spouse may improve your outlook on your marriage as well as provide health benefits.

Cuddling is a great way to share the gift of touch and experience oxytocin, also known as the love hormone.

When you are available to give or want to receive a cuddle, show your spouse the sign below and ask for a cuddle session.

Be willing to cuddle when your spouse asks for it to help keep the joy of cuddling alive in your marriage.

Share or make up a fantasy that involves your partner. Find handy relevant props to make the fantasy seem as real as possible.

Do make sure that the safety and willingness of your partner are taken care of during your fantasy play.

Take turns planning an evening of intimacy for your partner, where you serve as the host or hostess, and indulge your spouse in his or her favorite activities.

Strive to make your spouse feel that it is all about him or her on that special evening.

Being financially secure can take the stress out of many other aspects of your marriage.

Have a conversation with your spouse about what steps you could take together to improve or solidify your finances. Be sure to include how you want to use a small portion of it for travel and other activities while you save for the future.

Consider working with a financial planner if you need help to reach your financial goals.

Traveling is a great means of seeing how people around the world live.

What are your top three "must-see" places you want to visit in your lifetime?

*Next, share your lists of "must-see"
sites and commit now to plan the finances
and time off to make it happen.*

Going Forth in Love

Think about a major change that will probably happen to you within the next five years.

Discuss what support you would like from your spouse to help you deal with the change.

Listen to your partner's need for support and talk about the ways you can be supportive if the change occurs.

We can continue to evolve as spouses to help make our marriage stronger.

Consider one way you believe you could change to become a better partner for your spouse.

Share your beliefs with each other to see whether your partner would value this change.

Going Forth in Love

Have the two of you made plans for your next wedding anniversary?

If not, spend some time now making plans for a beautiful, memorable wedding anniversary celebration this year, even if it isn't a significant milestone.

If you are going to need some extra cash for your celebration, start setting aside a few dollars each pay period to make your dream celebration come true.

Congratulations – you've finished the Celebrating Your Love activities. Remember to keep finding ways to celebrate your marriage as the two of you go forth in love.

Reflect on the activities you enjoyed the most and which activities you'll want to practice more to continue growing your marriage.

Going Forth in Love

References

Preparing to Celebrate Our Love:

The Cleveland Clinic. (n.d.). Diseases and conditions. Retrieved from http://my.clevelandclinic.org/health/diseases_conditions/hic_Understanding_COPD/hic_Pulmonary_Rehabilitation_Is_it_for_You/hic_Diaphragmatic_Breathing

Bailey, E. (2016). Why breathing helps us relax. Retrieved from http://www.healthcentral.com/anxiety/c/1443/156561/breathing-helps/

Kelly, M. (2013, July 3). Exercise reorganizes the brain to be more resilient to stress. Retrieved from https://www.princeton.edu/main/news/archive/S37/28/70Q72/index.xml?section=topstories

Cherishing Our Past:

Morgan, A.L. (2014, July 24). 20 ways to refresh your marriage. [Slide show]. Retrieved from http://www.msn.com/en-us/lifestyle/marriage/20-ways-to-refresh-your-marriage/ss-AA3glNm#image=16

Universitaet Bielefeld. (2016, July 20). A chair for getting fit and trim. Retrieved from https://www.sciencedaily.com/releases/2016/07/160720094606.htm

Chapman, E. (2014, July 16). The science behind a great marriage. Retrieved from http://www.msn.com/enus/news/other/the-science-behind-a-great-marriage/ss-AA2Q7xg

Baldwin, M. (n.d.). The warm glow of the past. Retrieved from http://www.scienceofrelationships.com/home/2012/12/11/the-warm-glow-of-the-past.html

ASU News. (2007, January 5). Researcher studies benefits of reminiscing about laughter. Retrieved from http://www.news.appstate.edu/2007/01/05/research-11/

Checking the State Of Our Union:

Washburn, C & Christensen, D. (2008). Financial harmony: A key component of successful marriage relationship. Retrieved from https://ncsu.edu/ffci/publications/2008/v13-n1-2008-spring/Washburn-Christensen.php

Having Fun Together:

Foley, T. (2012). Cook your way toward a healthier marriage. Retrieved from http://www.focusonthefamily.ca/marriage/first-five-years/cook-your-way-toward-a-healthier-marriage

Healthy Living. (2013, February 9). The perfect workout partner: Why couples who sweat together stay together. Retrieved from http://www.huffingtonpost.com/2013/02/09/workout-partner-healthy-couples-valentinesday_n_2638571.html

Gordon, A. (2012, January 9). Couples who play together stay together. Retrieved from http://berkeleysciencereview.com/couples-who-play-together-stay-together/

Jayson, S. (2008, July 16). Married couples who play together stay together. Retrieved from http://usatoday30.usatoday.com/news/nation/2008-07-15-fun-in-marriage_N.htm

Marano, H.E. (2003, April 29). The benefits of laughter. Retrieved from https://www.psychologytoday.com/articles/200304/the-benefits-laughter

Heid, M. (2014, November 19). You asked: Does laughing have real health benefits? Retrieved from http://time.com/3592134/laughing-health-benefits/

Pedersen, T. (2015). Why nature is so good for your mental health. [Blog post]. Retrieved from http://psychcentral.com/blog/archives/2015/10/08/why-nature-is-so-good-for-your-mental-health/

Andrews, L.W. (2011, April 10). Kite flying for health and happiness. [Blog post]. Retrieved from https://www.sychologytoday.com/blog/minding-the-body/201104/kite-flying-health-and-happiness

Society for Personality and Social Psychology. (2014, February 10).Keep romance alive with double dates. Retrieved from https://www.sciencedaily.com/releases/2014/02/140210114544.htm

Lebowitz, S. (2016, August 15). There's an easy way to keep the romance alive in your relationship, but you'll have to leave the house. Retrieved from http://www.businessinsider.com/couples-who-try-new-things-together-are-happier-2016-8

Miller, A. (2013). Can this marriage be saved? Retrieved from https://www.apa.org/monitor/2013/04/marriage.aspx

Parker-Pope, T. (2008, February 12). Reinventing date night for long-married couples. Retrieved from http://www.nytimes.com/2008/02/12/health/12well.html

Brigham Young University (2013, March 21). Parents should do chores together, study says. Retrieved from https://www.sciencedaily.com/releases/2013/03/130321093104.htm

Appreciating Each Other:

Gottman, J.M. & J. (2011, January 3). How to keep love going strong. Retrieved from http://www.yesmagazine.org/issues/what-happy-families-know/how-to-keep-love-going-strong

Communicating Our Love

Hagen, S. (2014, January 31). Divorce rate cut in half for couples who discussed relationship movies. Retrieved from https://www.rochester.edu/news/divorce-rate-cut-in-half-for-couples-who-discussed-relationship-movies/

Rogge, R. D., Cobb, R. J.,Lawrence, E., Johnson, M. D., Bradbury, T. N.(2013). Is skills training necessary for the primary prevention of marital distress and dissolution? A 3-year experimental study of three interventions. *Journal of Consulting and Clinical Psychology*, 81(6), 949-961. http://dx.doi.org/10.1037/a0034209

Being Intimate Together:

P. M. (2010, June 19). Romantic songs make women more open to dates.[Blog post]. Retrieved from https://noustuff.wordpress.com/2010/06/19/romantic-songs-make-women-more-open-to-dates/

Whitbourne, S.K. (2012, July 24). The kiss of health. [Blog post]. Retrieved from https://www.psychologytoday.com/blog/fulfillment-any-age/201207/the-kiss-health

Horan, S.M. (2014, March 31). The surprising benefits of kissing. [Blog post]. Retrieved https://www.psychologytoday.com/blog/adventures-in-dating/201403/the-surprising-benefits-kissing

WebMd (n.d.). In plain sight: Kissing chemistry. [Slide show]. Retrieved from http://www.webmd.com/a-to-zguides/video/heat-stroke

Brittle, Z. (2014, May 28). K is for kissing. [Blog post]. Retrieved from https://www.gottman.com/blog/k-is-for-kissing/
McConnell, A.R. (2016, August 16). Hugs and warm touches benefit health and well-being. [Blog post]. Retrieved from

https://www.psychologytoday.com/blog/the-social-self/201608/hugs-and-warm-touches-benefit-health-and-wellbeing

Horan, S.M. (2016, July 29). Are you getting enough affection from your partner? [Blog post]. Retrieved from https://www.psychologytoday.com/blog/adventures-in-dating/201607/are-you-getting-enough-affection-your-partner

Hickok, H. (2014, October 28). How to fall back in love with your husband. Retrieved from http://www.redbookmag.com/love-sex/relationships/a19288/fall-back-in-love/

Gottman, J.M. & J. (n.d.) How to keep love going strong. Retrieved from http://www.stlcw.com/Handouts/How_To_Keep_Love_Going_Strong.pdf

Degges-White, S. (2015, November 24). 5 Resolutions for enhancing intimate relationships. [Blog post].Retrieved from https://www.psychologytoday.com/blog/lifetime-connections/201511/5-resolutions-enhancing-intimaterelationships?collection=1086082

Photo and Image Attribution:
All photos and images were obtained from Shutterstock.com

About the Author

ELLE DAHLMAN has a Master of Arts in Clinical Psychology from the University of California, Berkeley, where her studies included family relationships and the psychology of optimism. She loves using her background in psychology to inspire others.

She is working to increase the set of titles published under the Drawing Closer Together™ series, to help people on their journey of togetherness from dating to marriage to growing a family to living a full life.

Elle also is a writer and speaker on topics related to education, learning, and marketing technology. She lives in the Midwest with her wonderful husband and two delightful boys.

Elle wants to hear from you.

Twitter: @InwardVistas   Facebook: @InwardVistas

Email: ElleDahlman@InwardVistas.com

Email list: Subscribe@InwardVistas.com

Also by Elle Dahlman

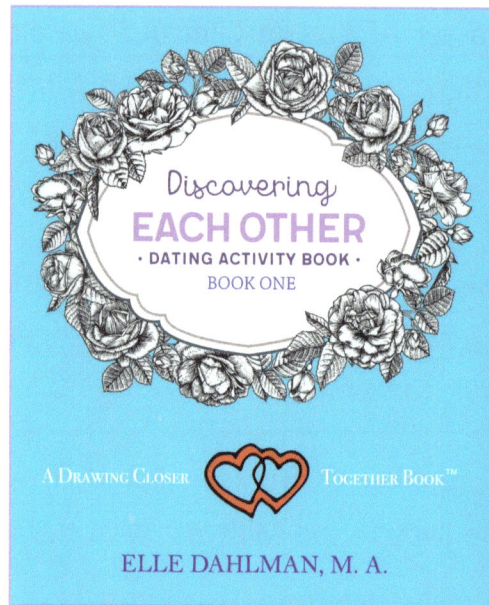

The Discovering Each Other Dating Activity Book - Book One is full of drawing, coloring and playful activities for dating couples. It can help you get more comfortable with your date with easy to do activities that help break the ice.

The activities you and your date will do can help dating couples learn more about each other in a enjoyable manner. There are also games in which you work together or challenge each other to accomplish a goal, and hopefully, bond together as you complete them.

The book combines easy to fill in coloring pages, fun games and a few simple drawing activities. The book is designed to help you speed up how much and how quickly you learn about each other. The book is available at Amazon.com.

Learn more about **Discovering Each Other Dating Activity Book - Book One** at Amazon.com or the Inward Vistas website at www.InwardVistas.com.

www.ingramcontent.com/pod-product-compliance
Lightning Source LLC
Chambersburg PA
CBHW042022080426

42735CB00003B/133